IS THIS THE END?

A 30-Day Devotional for Those Losing or Lost Loved Ones

Is This the End?

— A 30-Day Devotional for Those Losing or Lost
Loved Ones —

Erick Hurt

**GOSPEL
SUPPORT**
PUBLISHING

Why One Devotional a Day?

This devotional was intentionally designed to be read **one lesson per day**—not because the content is lengthy, but because the goal is depth. True spiritual transformation rarely comes from quickly consuming truth; it comes from slowing down and allowing the Holy Spirit to do His work in the heart.

Each day's reading is meant to be meditated on, prayed through, and lived out. The reflection questions are included not to fill time, but to create space for meditation, clarity, and honest response. When we rush past truth, we often miss its transforming power. When we slow down, the Lord has room to reveal, renew, and refine.

This pace also provides an opportunity to grow in self-control—one of the beautiful fruits of the Spirit (Galatians 5:22–23). Resisting the urge to move ahead, even when it's "just one more," cultivates the maturity and patience needed for a healthy walk with Christ. So resist the urge to hurry. Take your time. Let each day's lesson linger.

Using This Devotional in a Group Setting

This 30-day devotional was designed not only for personal growth, but also to support group study and discussion. If you're going through this with a small group, Bible study, or church class, you'll find a simple **Leader's Guide** at the back of this book.

The Leader's Guide includes:

- A suggested weekly group format
- Discussion prompts for each devotional
- Application questions to help your group reflect and respond
- Space for additional notes and insights

Whether you're leading two people or twenty, this guide will help you keep the focus on Christ and make space for real connection and transformation.

Table of Contents

Dear friend,

Is This the End?
A 30-Day Devotional for Those Losing or Lost Loved Ones

Grief has a way of stopping time. One moment life feels familiar, and the next, everything changes. A phone call. A diagnosis. A final breath. And suddenly you're left with questions you never wanted to ask. *Why did this happen? Where are they now? Is this the end?*

This devotional was written for that place.

Throughout the Bible, God meets people in their deepest sorrow—not with shallow answers, but with His presence, His promises, and His Son. From the tears of Job to the tomb of Lazarus, from the cross to the empty grave, the Bible speaks honestly about loss while pointing relentlessly to hope.

This 30-day devotional will walk with you through grief one day at a time, anchoring your heart in the truth of the gospel. You'll be reminded that God is near to the brokenhearted, that Jesus entered our suffering, and that death does not get the last word.

If you're numb, angry, exhausted, confused, or simply trying to survive the day, you are not alone. This journey is not about fixing your grief or rushing your healing. It's about meeting Christ in the middle of your sorrow and discovering that even here, He is faithful.

My prayer is that as you move through these pages, you will find space to grieve honestly, permission to heal slowly, and confidence to hope again. Not because the pain disappears, but because Jesus is present—and He has already conquered death.

Each day includes:

- A title that gives language to what you may be feeling
- A Scripture passage to anchor you in truth
- A short devotional grounded in the gospel
- A prayer to help you bring your sorrow to God
- Reflection questions to gently guide your heart

This journey is not about pretending everything is okay. It's about learning to trust God when life feels broken. It's about discovering that grief is not the end of your story—because there is new life through Jesus' resurrection.

Take this one day at a time. There is no timeline, no pressure, and no expectation beyond showing up honestly before God. Let the truth of the gospel meet you where you are, hold you in your sorrow, and carry you toward the hope that is coming.

Because in Christ, this is not the end.
It's the beginning of forever.

Day 1 – Is This the End?

Truth for Today: John 11:25

Jesus said to her, "I am the resurrection and the life. The one who believes in me will live, even though they die."

This is your hope—even here, in the middle of all your sorrow, suffering, and questioning. Why did God take them? Why is this happening to me? Everything changed in an instant. Complete silence with their final breath. It felt like time stood still. My heart sank—when their heart stopped. Life would never be the same—forever changed.

You look around and wonder how everyone else can go on like nothing happened. Your heart is broken, your life is shattered, scarred, and standing still. Thoughts are racing through your mind;

Is this the end?

Mary and Martha asked the same questions. Their brother Lazarus was gone. They sent word to Jesus, but when He received the news of his friend's death, He didn't come right away. And when He finally arrived, it was too late. Lazarus had died and the family was crushed.

"Lord, if You had been here, he wouldn't have died..." (John 11:21).

Behind their words we find our questions. Why didn't You come in time? Where were You when I needed You? Why is this happening to me? And what does Jesus say? He doesn't give a speech, or a timeline, nor an explanation, He gives the family Himself.

"I am the resurrection and the life."

In other words, you think this is "the end", but I am the One who will overcome death, and give my life for the world. Jesus doesn't deny the pain of loss, He drew closer and wept with them. He shared in their sorrow. And then, in the silence, suffering, and through His own tears Jesus calls Lazarus out of the tomb. Revealing that His presence and power are stronger than the grave.

That's the same Jesus who's with you today. Maybe you're still in shock. Maybe you feel numb, angry, or confused. Maybe it feels like God has failed you, but He hasn't, and this is not the end of the story. In Christ, death doesn't get the final word, because He is the resurrection—and He is life. And, *"The one who believes in me will live, even though they die."*

Prayer

Jesus, I feel lost in this grief. I don't know what to say or even how to pray. But You are the resurrection and the life. Thank You for drawing near to me in my time of need. Remind me that death isn't the end of our life. Help me to remember that You are the way, the truth, and the life.

Reflection Questions

1. How does this story encourage your heart that, in Christ, this is not the end?

_____

_____

_____

_____

_____

2. What does it mean to you that Jesus draws near and weeps with those who grieve?

_____

_____

_____

_____

_____

3. What questions are you carrying that you haven't been able to speak out loud yet?

_____

_____

_____

_____

_____

_____

_____

_____

_____

Day 2

Day 2 – When the Tears Don't Stop

Truth for Today: Psalm 56:8

"You have kept count of my tossings; put my tears in your bottle. Are they not in your book?"

You didn't expect to hurt like this, cry this long, or the pain to run this deep. It hits you out of nowhere, while driving, doing dishes, folding laundry. Sometimes it hits you seeing an old photo, smelling a familiar scent, or hearing a song that strikes your heart.

The tears come streaming, and they keep falling. You might think, shouldn't I be stronger than this? Grief doesn't follow the rules. It comes in waves, unexpected, overwhelming, and overflowing. And yet, God meets you there with comfort and compassion. He sees every tear. But He doesn't just see them, He holds them for you.

Psalm 56:8 says He puts your tears in a bottle. That's not just a quote filled with passion, it's personal care from His heart to yours. And your pain matters to God. Every tear is counted. Every restless night is recorded. Your sorrow isn't wasted or unseen. It's sacred to the One who gave you life. God didn't just watch your pain from a distance, He stepped into it, and lived it.

In Jesus, the Son of God became "the man of sorrows, acquainted with grief" (Isaiah 53:3). He wept at the tomb of His friend. He cried out in anguish in the Garden—because the burden and sorrow were too great. On the cross, He bore not only the weight of your sin, but the weight of your sorrow. He took death head-on, and rose again on the third day.

Grief may flood your heart now, but Christ has already secured a future. Where there will be no more mourning or death. And where every tear will be wiped away (Revelation 21:4).

But until that day, He holds your tears in His bottle. Purchased by the wounds in His hands and feet. Proof of His love and compassion for you. And one day you will see Him face to face and He will personally wipe that final tear from your eyes with His nail-scarred hands.

Prayer

Jesus, You know what it means to weep. You cried, You suffered, and You died for me. Thank You for not turning away from my pain but carrying me through it. Help me to see that my tears are safe with You, and that because of Your resurrection, this sorrow will one day give way to joy.

Reflection Questions

1. What stands out to you about the truth that Jesus understands sorrow from the inside, not from a distance?

_____

_____

_____

_____

_____

2. Where do you feel the weight of grief most strongly right now—emotionally, physically, or spiritually?

_____

_____

_____

_____

_____

3. What might it look like to simply bring that grief into Christ's presence today, without trying to fix it?

_____

_____

_____

_____

_____

_____

_____

_____

_____

_____

_____

_____

Day 3 – Numbness, Anger, Silence

Truth for Today: Job 3:11

"Why did I not perish at birth, and die as I came from the womb?"

There comes a moment in grief when you feel... nothing.

You're not even sure how to describe it. The world keeps moving, people keep talking, and you're still breathing—but inside, everything feels shut down. Numb. Or angry. Or just... silent.

You may feel guilty for not crying. Or guilty for yelling at God. You may wonder if you're "doing it wrong"—that you should feel something different, say something more spiritual, or hold yourself together for everyone else.

But look at Job.

He lost everything—his children, his health, his livelihood, and his sense of purpose. And what did he do? He broke. He cursed the day he was born. He asked, *"Why did I not perish at birth?"* He sat in silence. He groaned. He wept.

And still... God did not reject him.

Is This the End?

Job's honesty was not condemned in the story—not because he handled grief perfectly, but because he brought his grief honestly to God. He did not sanitize his sorrow or hide his pain behind religious words.

You don't need to muster up your strength with God. God is not threatened by raw emotion. He is not offended by your anger or put off by your silence. He invites you to bring it all—and meets you there.

Job even longed for someone to stand between him and God—someone who could place a hand on both and bring peace.

"If only there were someone to mediate between us, someone to bring us together" (Job 9:33).

Job did not yet see how God would answer that cry. But the gospel tells us that God Himself would provide what Job longed for.

In Jesus Christ, we are given a Mediator. Jesus entered our world of pain and sorrow and took our place. On the cross, He carried the weight of sin and suffering—in obedience and love for you. Because He stands between us and God, our grief is no longer faced alone.

If you're numb, Jesus does not pull away.
If you're angry, He does not scold you.
If you're silent, He still draws near.

He is with you in your grief. And because He has already walked the road of sorrow, you can trust Him to walk with you—through the pain and into His healing arms.

Prayer

Father, I don't have the words right now. I'm numb. Maybe angry. Maybe I'm too tired to care. Thank You for not turning away from me. Thank You for giving me Jesus, who meets me where I am and does not abandon me in my sorrow. Help me trust that You are near, even when I feel nothing at all.

Reflection Questions

1. What emotions—or lack of emotion—have surprised you most in your grief so far?

_____

_____

_____

_____

2. What would it look like to bring those feelings honestly before God, without trying to correct or control them?

_____

_____

_____

_____

3. How does knowing that Jesus cried out in suffering help you feel less alone in this moment?

_____

_____

_____

_____

_____

_____

_____

_____

_____

_____

_____

_____

Day 4 – Jesus Wept Too

Truth for Today: John 11:35

"Jesus wept."

---

*I*t's the shortest verse in the Bible, but maybe one of the most powerful—Jesus wept. He didn't weep because He was powerless. He didn't cry because He didn't have a plan. He knew He would raise Lazarus from the dead.

And yet... He still stood outside the tomb and cried for His friend. Why? Because Jesus doesn't just fix pain, He enters it with us. He shares it. And He feels it too.

This moment in John 11 shows us the heart of our Savior. He wasn't cold or distant. He wasn't emotionless or unaffected. He was deeply moved by the sorrow of His friends.

Jesus wept because death hurts. Jesus wept because His friends were mourning loss. Jesus wept because Lazarus was His friend. Jesus wept because love thinks of others and mourns with them.

And that means your tears don't push God away, they draw Him close, to comfort, counsel, and weep with you. You may wonder if your sadness is a lack of faith. You may feel ashamed for crying again, or worried that others are growing tired of your tears.

But Jesus proves that sorrow and faith live in the same heart. He didn't hide His tears, and neither should you. Even more, this moment reveals something meaningful, Jesus didn't just weep about death, He wept about losing a friend.

He walked toward the tomb to call Lazarus out. And He walked out of His own tomb on your behalf. He went to the cross to bear the curse of sin and death. And by His resurrection, He silenced the grave while securing *"eternal life"* for those who trust Him.

So when you stand at the edge of loss, remember, you follow a Savior who weeps with you, who died for you, who rose for you, and who always walks with you in your darkest days.

Grief is heavy and the tears may keep falling. But Jesus isn't standing far off waiting for you to move on. He's kneeling beside you, sharing in your sorrow, and wiping your tears. The One with the nail-scarred hands is reminding you that your loved ones will rise again.

Prayer

Jesus, thank You for weeping. You didn't hide Your tears, and I don't need to hide mine. Thank You for feeling sorrow so deeply, and for entering mine with love. Thank You for being near to me in my grief. Help me see that my tears, You will one day wipe away forever.

Reflection Questions

1. How does it comfort you to know that Jesus wept at the grave of His friend?

_____

_____

_____

_____

_____

2. In what ways have you felt pressure to hide your grief?

_____

_____

_____

_____

_____

3. What would it look like to bring your tears to Jesus rather than away from Him?

_____

_____

_____

_____

_____

_____

_____

_____

_____

_____

_____

_____

Day 5 – Grief Is Not a Lack of Faith

Truth for Today: 1 Thessalonians 4:13

"Brothers and sisters, we do not want you to be uninformed about those who sleep in death, so that you do not grieve like the rest of mankind, who have no hope."

---

*S*ome people will tell you to "stay strong." Others will urge you to "move on." Some might even suggest that if you really trusted God, you wouldn't be so emotional. Or that "God's going to use this for good." These are all well-meaning people struggling to find words of comfort for you.

It's just poor timing for your broken heart.

But the Bible says something incredible here. Paul doesn't say, "Don't grieve." He says, "Don't grieve like those who have no hope."

That means grieve and still believe. To mourn deeply and hold onto eternal hope. To cry in and through pain, and yet trust that Christ has conquered the grave. Grief is not a sign of weakness. It's not a failure of faith. It's evidence that your love is real, and that loss still hurts in a fallen world.

Jesus wept. The early church wept. Paul wept. Why? Because the sting of death is painful. It pierces the heart, even for those who believe in the resurrection. But here's the difference—we do not grieve as those who *"have no hope."*

Our tears fall with the confidence that death doesn't win. Our sorrow rests on a greater promise, that Jesus rose from the grave and is now seated in heaven. And those who die in Him will rise too.

The gospel doesn't remove grief, it redeems it through His resurrection. It tells us that death is not the end, and loss is not forever. It reminds us that Jesus entered death so that He could bring us through it. And when He returns, the dead in Christ will rise first, and we will be reunited with them in His presence forever (1 Thess. 4:16–17).

So grieve. Let the tears come. Sit in the sadness. You don't have to pretend everything is okay. But in your grief, remember that you have hope because you believe that Jesus died and rose again!

Prayer

Father, I don't want to grieve like the world does—without hope. But I also can't ignore how much this hurts. Thank You that Jesus died and rose again, so I can trust that death doesn't get the victory. Help me to grieve honestly, but with confidence in Your promise of resurrection.

Reflection Questions

1. In what ways have you felt pressure—spoken or unspoken—to hide your grief?

_____

_____

_____

_____

_____

2. What might it look like for you to hold grief in one hand and hope in the other today?

_____

_____

_____

_____

_____

Is This the End?

3. How does knowing that Jesus rose from the dead bring comfort, even if the pain remains?

_____

_____

_____

_____

_____

_____

_____

_____

_____

_____

_____

_____

_____

Day 6 – The News That Changed Everything

Truth for Today: Psalm 46:1–2

"God is our refuge and strength, an ever-present help in trouble. Therefore we will not fear, though the earth give way and the mountains fall into the heart of the sea."

You remember exactly where you were and what you were doing. The call. The knock. The moment the words were spoken—like a punch to the gut. Like the ground dropped out from beneath your feet. In an instant, everything changed. That kind of moment doesn't fade easily but can linger, even years later.

Sometimes it replays in your mind like a movie you didn't choose to watch. Sometimes it haunts your sleep, tightens your chest, or takes your breath away. You may feel like you're walking around in a world that doesn't even feel real anymore. When your world falls apart, it can seem like nothing is stable.

But Psalm 46 meets you in this very place, in that very moment, in all the mourning. God is our refuge and strength, an ever-present help in trouble. Not a future help, nor a distant helper, but He is present. He is here, right now, in the worst moment of your life. He draws near, even if you can't feel Him.

Is This the End?

The psalm says, "though the earth gives way…" That's what grief feels like, doesn't it? Like the solid ground of your life has crumbled. What once felt permanent is gone. What once felt safe now feels shattered.

Even if the ground moves, you can find stability—because Jesus is your Rock and Refuge. The One who already entered the sorrow of this world—took on flesh, went to the cross, lived through pain and suffering, and rose again. When the world delivered news that crushed you, God already delivered Good News that holds you.

Christ died—but conquered death. And He is with you in this painful moment, not as a reminder, but as your Redeemer. You may not be ready to sing, and that's okay. You may not feel strong, and that's okay too. But you can collapse into the arms of the One who is your Refuge—your Rock—and your Redeemer.

Prayer

God, everything changed in that one moment. I still feel shaken. But You are my refuge and strength, my shelter when nothing else makes sense. Hold me up when I can't stand. Remind me that even if everything falls, You remain. Thank You, Jesus, for holding me steady with Your love.

Reflection Questions

1. What memories or moments still feel especially heavy for you, and what would it look like to bring them honestly before God?

_____

_____

_____

_____

_____

2. What does it mean to you that God is described as a refuge when everything feels unstable?

_____

_____

_____

_____

_____

3. How does knowing that Jesus entered suffering—and overcame death—offer even a small sense of stability right now?

_____

_____

_____

_____

_____

_____

_____

_____

_____

_____

_____

_____

_____

Day 7 – I Don't Know How to Pray Right Now

Truth for Today: Romans 8:26

"Likewise the Spirit helps us in our weakness. For we do not know what to pray for as we ought, but the Spirit himself intercedes for us with groanings too deep for words."

---

*Y*ou want to pray… but you don't know how.

You sit in silence, staring at the ceiling or clutching a tear-soaked pillow—and nothing comes out. Maybe you whisper, "God, help me," or maybe you just let the tears fall.

And that's okay.

Grief has a way of silencing us. It jumbles our thoughts and scrambles our words. You may feel like you're failing spiritually because you can't string together a decent prayer—but God doesn't measure your faith by your vocabulary. He doesn't need polished phrases. He doesn't require perfect speeches.

He hears your groans. And more than that—*He intercedes* for you in them.

Romans 8:26 says the Holy Spirit Himself intercedes for you. When you can't find the words, the Spirit speaks for you, with groans deeper than words. Not formal prayers, not wordy statements, but through groans. Real, deep pain lifted up to the Father on your behalf. And this is the gospel's promise—the One interceding for you is the same Spirit who raised Jesus from the dead (Romans 8:11).

Because Christ died and rose for you, the Holy Spirit was sent to dwell in you. He doesn't abandon you when you've lost a loved one. He draws close, to comfort you, to counsel you, and to guide you.. Right now, in the cloud of grief, He is with you.

The Spirit is crying out with you and for you. And right now, at the right hand of the Father—Jesus is also interceding for you (Romans 8:34).

You are held by a God who prays when you cannot. So take it all in, and if all you can do is sit in silence, sit with Jesus. If all you can do is cry, cry in His presence. Let Him carry what you cannot express.

Prayer

Father, I don't have the words. My heart is heavy, and my thoughts are scattered. But I know You are still with me. Thank You that the Holy Spirit prays for me when I cannot. Thank You that Jesus still intercedes for me because of His finished work on the cross. Help me to rest, even when I can't speak.

Reflection Questions

1. In what ways have you felt ashamed or discouraged because you didn't know how to pray?

_____

_____

_____

_____

_____

2. How does it change your view of prayer to know the Spirit intercedes for you?

_____

_____

_____

_____

_____

3. What would it look like to simply rest in God's presence today?

_____

_____

_____

_____

_____

_____

_____

_____

_____

_____

_____

_____

_____

Day 8 – Could I Have Done More?

Truth for Today: Ecclesiastes 3:1–2

"There is a time for everything, and a season for every activity under the heavens: a time to be born and a time to die…"

---

*G*uilt has a way of sneaking into grief. You replay conversations you wish had gone differently. You remember what you said, or didn't say. You think of things you could've done better, more intentionally. And the questions begin, could I have done better?

Maybe you carry regret from years ago. Maybe you feel like you missed something. Or maybe you were there, fully present, but now your mind keeps accusing you anyway.

Grief and guilt often hold hands, but they are not the same. Guilt doesn't heal grief. It makes it heavier. That's why today's Bible passage reminds us that our lives are in God's hands. There is a time to be born and a time to die.

You are not the author of someone else's story. You didn't write their beginning, and you couldn't control their end. There's freedom in accepting that you were never meant to carry what only God could.

And here's where the gospel meets your regret. Jesus not only died for your sin, but for your regrets, your failures, and your shortcomings. He conquered death to bring comfort, counsel, and guidance.

But even if you truly failed, there is grace. If you were imperfect, there is mercy. If you did your best but still feel it's not enough, there is rest.

While on the cross, Jesus cried, "It is finished." That wasn't just about salvation—it was about the end of striving… the end of self-condemnation… and the end of thinking you have to fix everything.

He died to cancel your not-enoughs. And His grace is sufficient.

So if you find yourself grieving and feeling guilty, bring both of them to Jesus. You can mourn what's been lost and trust the One who restores you. You can release your regrets into the hands of a Savior who knows the full story—and still loves you beyond words.

Prayer

Jesus, You know my heart. You know the things I wish I could change. I can't go back, but I can come to You. Thank You for dying for my sins and my shortcomings. Help me to trust Your grace over my guilt and Your love over my regret. Help me to rest in what You've already finished.

Reflection Questions

1. What regrets or "what ifs" tend to surface most often in your grief?

_____

_____

_____

_____

_____

2. How does remembering that life and death rest in God's hands affect the way you carry that guilt?

_____

_____

_____

_____

_____

3. What would it look like to place those regrets into Jesus' care today?

_____

_____

_____

_____

_____

_____

_____

_____

_____

_____

_____

_____

Day 9 – Why Did God Let This Happen?

Truth for Today: Isaiah 55:8–9

"For my thoughts are not your thoughts, neither are your ways my ways," declares the Lord. "As the heavens are higher than the earth, so are my ways higher than your ways and my thoughts than your thoughts."

---

*W*hy? It's the question that echoes through the silence. The one you ask at night when no one else is around. Why did this happen? Why now? Why them? Why didn't You stop it, God? And maybe… no answer has been given, no answer has come.

Isaiah 55 doesn't give us a simple explanation, but it does give us a deeper perspective. God sees what we don't. His thoughts are higher. His ways are greater. We live within the limits of time, space, and pain. But God operates from eternity, knowing the whole story from beginning to end.

But that doesn't cancel the aches and pains of loss. It does, however, remind us that even when we can't understand what God is doing, we can still trust who He is.

When Jesus hung on the cross, the people watching must have asked, why is this happening? It looked like defeat. It looked like injustice. But it was the greatest act of love the world has ever known. God took what looked like the end, and turned it into eternity.

If God can use a cross and bring life through resurrection, He can use this pain for a purpose. You may not see it yet. You may never understand it fully on this side of eternity. But the God who gave His own Son for you will never waste your suffering.

He will never leave you in it alone. You are allowed to ask why. You are allowed to wrestle, cry, and not have answers. But don't stop there. Bring your "why" to the foot of the cross, and let Jesus meet you there with His love and compassion.

What looked like the darkest moment in history became the brightest hope the world has ever known. The cross reminds us that when God seems most absent, He is often doing His deepest work. If He did not spare His own Son but gave Him up for us, we can trust that even this pain is not forgotten, not meaningless, and won't be wasted.

Prayer

God, I don't understand why this happened. I don't see what You see. But I choose to believe that Your thoughts are higher than mine, and Your love is deeper than my pain. Help me trust You in the mystery. Thank You for Jesus—who turns sorrow into hope and death into life.

Reflection Questions

1. Have you found yourself asking God "why" in this season of grief?

_____

_____

_____

_____

_____

2. How does the cross help you trust God even when His ways feel hidden?

_____

_____

_____

_____

_____

3. What would it look like to trust His heart when you can't see His hand?

_____

_____

_____

_____

_____

_____

_____

_____

_____

_____

_____

_____

Day 10 – If Only...

Truth for Today: John 11:21

"Martha said to Jesus, "Lord, if only you had been here, my brother would not have died."

---

*E*arlier in this devotional, we looked at the moment Jesus came to Mary and Martha after their brother Lazarus had died—the moment when He declared, "I am the resurrection and the life." But there's another part of that same story worth slowing down for—the ache of "if only."

"If only I had called sooner..."
"If only they'd gone to the doctor..."
"If only I'd said I love you one more time..."
"If only God had done something..."

Martha knew the pain of "if only." Her brother, Lazarus, was dead. She had watched him grow sick, had sent word to Jesus, had waited, and Jesus didn't show up. Not in time, anyway.

When He finally arrived, her words spilled out, "Lord, if only You had been here, my brother would not have died." Honest, direct, and unfiltered. And Jesus didn't correct her. He didn't scold her for questioning or grieving or feeling disappointed. He received her sorrow, and then He gave her

Is This the End?

something totally unexpected. He gave her a promise. *"I am the resurrection and the life…"* (John 11:25).

At that moment, Jesus didn't explain the delay. He didn't answer all her questions. But He gave her Himself—the One who defeats death.

If you're living with the ache of if only, know this:

Jesus is not angry with your questions. He's not disappointed in your doubts. He is the Savior who draws near to those who mourn, and reminds them that the grave is not the end.

No matter what didn't happen, no matter what you wish had happened—Jesus has already done what you needed most. He went to the cross. He bore your pain and suffering. He entered death… and walked out of the tomb alive.

You may carry sorrow, regret, or questions that feel unresolved—but the cross proves: that Jesus loves you even in the heartache. And the resurrection proves: that death doesn't win.

So bring your "if only" to Jesus. Rest in the promise of life after death. Rest in the promise that Jesus conquered death that we might live again. Rest in the promise that God so loved the world that He gave His one and only Son, *and whoever believes in Him shall not perish.*

Prayer

Jesus, I have so many "if only" thoughts. I wish things had gone differently. But thank You for not turning away from my questions. Thank You for meeting me like You met Martha—with both compassion and truth. Help me to trust that You are the resurrection and the life, even when my heart aches.

Reflection Questions

1. What "if only" has been weighing on your heart lately?

_____

_____

_____

_____

2. How does Jesus' response to Martha show His compassion in grief?

_____

_____

_____

_____

3. What would it look like to trust His promise more than your pain?

_____

_____

_____

_____

_____

_____

_____

_____

_____

_____

_____

_____

Day 11 – What Happens After Death?

Truth for Today: 2 Corinthians 5:8

"We are confident, I say, and would prefer to be away from the body and at home with the Lord."

What happens when someone dies? It's a question that haunts the grieving heart. Whether you were in the room when they passed or miles away, the reality of death raises deep, urgent thoughts. Where are they now? Are they okay? What did they see at that moment?

Paul answers the question with confidence—not guesswork. He says that for those who are in Christ, to be absent from the body is to be present with the Lord.

Not asleep.
Not floating in darkness.
Not stuck in a waiting pattern.
Present—with Jesus.

There's no delay, no purgatory, and no confusion in eternity for the one who belongs to Christ. The moment you take your last breath, your spirit is welcomed into the presence of the Savior who defeated death.

This truth isn't just theology—it's comfort and care. Jesus told the thief on the cross, "Today you will be with Me in paradise" (Luke 23:43).

That's how immediate and personal our hope is. And that same hope is yours—and your loved one's if they've trusted in Him. It's available right now for anyone who will receive Christ by faith.

And the reason we can believe this with confidence isn't because we've earned or deserved it—but because Jesus paid for it. He died to forgive your sin and rose from the grave to defeat death—forever!

The resurrection is God's announcement that the grave is not the end, but a new beginning. If you're wondering what happened in that final moment, or aching to know where your loved one went—let the Bible speak loud and clear: *to be absent from the body is to be present with the Lord.*

In Christ, death is a doorway, not a dead end. It's the moment we step into the arms of the One who says, "Welcome home."

Prayer

Lord, death feels so final. But thank You that in Christ, it's not the end. Thank You for the promise that to be absent from the body is to be present with You. Help me rest in that truth, and to remember that You have overcome the grave.

Reflection Questions

    1.   What emotions rise in you when you think about what happens after death?

_____

_____

_____

_____

_____

    2.   How does the gospel give you confidence about your own life after death, and the life of others?

_____

_____

_____

_____

_____

3. Where do you find yourself trusting Jesus as the One who conquered death on your behalf?

_____

_____

_____

_____

_____

_____

_____

_____

_____

_____

_____

_____

Day 12 – Are They in Heaven?

Truth for Today: Luke 23:43

"Jesus answered him, 'Truly I tell you, today you will be with me in paradise.'"

---

*L*ooking at the cross, you see Jesus hanging between two criminals. One of them asked to be remembered. And you may find yourself wondering—*are they in heaven?* It's the question you might not say out loud, but it stirs in your heart.

Maybe they weren't churchgoers. Maybe they made a profession of faith long ago but drifted. Maybe they were the kind of person who prayed when they needed something, but struggled in faith.

And now you wonder. Where are they? Did they make it? We don't always know what happens in someone's final moments. But Jesus gives us a glimpse of His mercy in one of the most surprising conversations in the Bible.

A criminal, crucified next to Christ, gasping for breath, with no chance to turn his life around. No time to make amends. No good works left to offer. All he had was a desperate cry:

"Jesus, remember me…"

And Jesus answered him, *"Today you will be with Me in paradise."* What kind of Savior says that to a dying thief? A loving and merciful one, and this is our hope too. Salvation is not based on how well someone lived, but on whether they looked to Jesus.

Even at the last breath, mercy is available. We can't always know what took place in someone's heart before they died, but God does. He sees what we can't, and He is far more compassionate, patient, merciful, and loving than we are.

So what do you do when you don't know for sure? You trust the character of God. You trust the mercy of Christ. You release what you can't answer into the hands of the One who does all things right.

And if the weight of this question still crushes you, let it turn your heart toward what is certain, Jesus died for sinners. He saves those who call on Him, and He never turns away someone who believed in Him.

Prayer

Jesus, You see what I cannot. I don't know all that happened in their heart before the end—but You do. Thank You for being a Savior full of mercy, who welcomes even the desperate and the dying. Help me trust You with what I can't control and rest in the truth that You are always just and always good.

Reflection Questions

1. Have you been carrying anxiety about where your loved one is now?

_____

_____

_____

_____

_____

2. How does the thief on the cross help you see Jesus' mercy more clearly?

_____

_____

_____

_____

_____

3. What would it look like to release your unanswered
    questions into God's hands today?

_____

_____

_____

_____

_____

_____

_____

_____

_____

_____

_____

_____

Day 13 – What If They Weren't Saved?

Truth for Today: Genesis 18:25

"Will not the Judge of all the earth do right?"

$\mathcal{T}$his is the question many are afraid to say: *what if they weren't saved?* What if they never trusted in Jesus? What if they resisted faith? What if there was no fruit? What if…? It's a grief that goes deeper than sorrow—it feels like despair. Not just the pain of separation, but the fear of eternal loss.

If you're asking this question, you're not alone. Abraham once asked God if He would spare a city for the sake of a few righteous people. In that moment of tension between justice and mercy, Abraham anchored himself in this truth.

"Will not the Judge of all the earth do right?"

Here's what that means for you. God is perfectly just, and He is endlessly merciful. He never gets it wrong. He doesn't make hasty decisions. He doesn't miss anything. He sees every motive, every moment, and He always judges with perfect precision.

That may not answer every question, but it gives us something solid to stand on. You can trust God to do what is right with the soul of your loved one.

It's not your burden to carry. You weren't their Savior. You didn't write their story. But God knows it completely. And here's what the gospel reveals—God wants everyone to be saved.

He sent His Son not to condemn the world, but to save it through Him (John 3:17). He is patient, not wanting anyone to perish (2 Peter 3:9). The cross wasn't weak to save, it was deep and wide. And no one who turns to Christ—at any point—is turned away.

So what do you do with the pain of not knowing? You trust God's character. You remember that His mercy is greater than your imagination, but His justice is always perfect.

Let the weight of that question stir your heart toward urgency in sharing the gospel while there's still time. Let it humble you, not haunt you. Let it shape how you live now, not paralyze you with what you can't change. You can't rewrite the past, but you can trust the Author of life into the future.

Prayer

God, this is the question that haunts my heart. But I don't want to live in fear, I want to trust You. Thank You that You are both just and merciful. Help me to release this burden into Your hands and believe that You will always do what is right.

Reflection Questions

1. Have you been carrying fear or regret about the eternal state of someone you lost?

_____

_____

_____

_____

_____

2. What does Genesis 18:25 teach you about God's justice and mercy?

_____

_____

_____

_____

_____

3. How does the cross of Christ help you release what you cannot control?

_____

_____

_____

_____

_____

_____

_____

_____

_____

_____

_____

_____

_____

Day 14 – Will I Ever Be Myself Again?

Truth for Today: Psalm 147:3

"He heals the brokenhearted and binds up their wounds."

You don't feel like yourself anymore. You look in the mirror and see the same face, but everything inside feels different, numb, fragile, exhausted. You wonder if this grief has permanently altered you.

Will I ever laugh like I used to? Will the weight ever lift? Will I ever feel normal again? The truth is, grief does change us. It reshapes us. It wounds our hearts. It changes how we see the world. And in some ways, you won't go back to being the person you were before this loss.

But here's the hope of the gospel—God is not trying to return you to who you were. He's gently forming you into who He's making you to be.

Psalm 147:3 says the Lord heals the brokenhearted, not just covers up their pain or rushes them through it. He binds up wounds. That word pictures a careful, attentive healer, not ripping the bandage off, but tending to each layer with patience and love.

Your grief isn't ignored by God. It's seen, held, and slowly but tenderly, healed. And here's how we know He can

Is This the End?

do it—Jesus was broken for you. His death wasn't just about punishment and payment, it was about healing too. *By His wounds, we are healed* (Isaiah 53:5). He took your sin, your sorrow, your brokenness, and He rose again to make you new.

That doesn't mean your pain disappears overnight. But it does mean you are not beyond repair. Your life is not over. Your future is not ruined. And though you may feel different, you are still loved, completely secure, and gently being restored by the hands that were pierced for you.

You may never go back to "before." But God is always faithful in the "after." And piece by piece, He's building something beautiful in you.

Prayer

Father, I don't feel like myself anymore. This pain has changed me. But thank You for being the God who heals the brokenhearted. Bind up the places in me that feel too shattered to fix. Thank You that Jesus was broken so I could be made whole. Help me trust You to rebuild what I cannot.

Reflection Questions

1. In what ways has grief changed how you feel about yourself?

_____

_____

_____

_____

_____

2. What fears do you carry about the future?

_____

_____

_____

_____

_____

3. How does knowing Jesus was broken for you help you trust Him to heal you?

_____

_____

_____

_____

_____

_____

_____

_____

_____

_____

_____

Day 15 – The Empty Chair

Truth for Today: Psalm 23:4

"Even though I walk through the valley of the shadow of death, I will fear no evil, for you are with me…"

There it is. The chair they used to sit in.
At the table, in the living room, or on the porch.
It may be just wood and fabric, but now it holds a memory and an absence at the same time.

You glance toward it expecting to see them, hear them, laugh with them. But it's empty. And it hurts. Sometimes it stops you in your tracks. Sometimes it takes your breath away.

David, the psalmist, understood what it meant to walk through the valley of the shadow of death. He didn't pretend the valley wasn't dark. He didn't deny the pain, but he did proclaim something unshakable in the middle of it.

"You are with me."

The Shepherd doesn't leave when the valley gets deep. He doesn't wait for you on the other side—He walks with you through it. You may feel alone in the room, at the table, or on the couch—but you are never alone. And here's the truth—Jesus knows the pain of absence.

He stood at the grave of a friend and wept. He watched the crowds walk away. He was betrayed, abandoned, and forsaken. And on the cross, He cried out, "My God, My God, why have You forsaken Me?"—so that you would never be forsaken.

That empty chair reminds you of what you've lost, but the empty tomb reminds you of who is always with you. The Shepherd, Comforter, Counselor, and the One who restores your soul.

And one day, in the Kingdom of God, there will be another chair, one that is never empty. One where death has ended, and every tear is wiped away. A feast of reunion, joy, and the unending presence of Christ. That day is coming, but until then, the Shepherd is always by your side.

Prayer

Jesus, the empty spaces in my life speak louder than ever. I miss them. I long for their voice, their laugh, their presence. But thank You that You are always with me. Thank You for walking through my valley beside me.

Reflection Questions

1. What emotions rise up when you see the "empty chair" in your life?

_____

_____

_____

_____

_____

2. How does Psalm 23 remind you of God's presence even in painful places?

_____

_____

_____

_____

_____

3. What would it look like to invite Jesus into your moments of loneliness today?

_____

_____

_____

_____

_____

_____

_____

_____

_____

_____

_____

_____

Day 16 – What Do I Do With Their Things?

Truth for Today: Ecclesiastes 3:6

"A time to search and a time to give up, a time to keep and a time to throw away."

---

*Y*ou didn't realize how hard this part would be. In the closet, on the nightstand, or the dresser drawers. The jacket still hanging on the hook, or the scent still lingering in the fabric.

These aren't just "things"—they're pieces of your heart. Memories woven into the objects. Reminders of a life that touched yours. Now you're faced with a question that feels both practical and painful: what do I do with their things?

Ecclesiastes 3 reminds us that life unfolds in seasons. There is a time to keep, a time to treasure, a time to hold, a time to honor. And there is a time to let go, to release, to give, to move forward in freedom.

But the Bible doesn't give you a timeline. It gives you permission to walk this process slowly, and with the help of the Holy Spirit. There is no "right" time to box up clothes or photos. There's no shame in keeping some items forever, or in releasing them sooner than others might expect. This isn't about what others think. This is your time to grieve, so take as long as you need.

This is about letting God guide you, item by item, memory by memory, moment by moment. And the gospel meets your every need—so you don't need to cling to objects to cling to love.

Your loved one is not found in the sweater, the books, or the furniture. They are not gone because their things are gone. If they knew Christ, they are alive in His presence, and no item on earth is greater than knowing that. And if your heart still aches to hold onto something, Jesus understands. He knows what it is to love deeply, to share the memories, and to grieve in loss.

He also offers freedom, the kind that trusts, that love can outlast loss, and that hope isn't found in an empty room or chair, but in an empty tomb. After His resurrection, He ascended into heaven and is seated at God's right hand. And those who are in Christ are seated with Him (Ephesians 2:6).

So whether you keep it, give it away, or pass it along, do it with grace, not guilt. It's all temporary, really. The memories are more precious than the property—so let the Spirit guide your heart.

Prayer

Lord, this is harder than I expected. These things hold memories I'm afraid to lose. Help me know what to keep and what to let go. Lead me gently through each decision. Thank You that I don't have to hold onto things to hold onto love, and that in Christ, nothing is truly lost.

Reflection Questions

1. What item have you struggled the most to let go of and why?

_____

_____

_____

_____

2. How can you trust the Holy Spirit in this part of your grieving process?

_____

_____

_____

_____

3. Are there any physical "keepsakes" you could turn into spiritual reminders of God's faithfulness?

_____

_____

_____

_____

_____

_____

_____

_____

_____

_____

_____

Day 17 – Memories and Unexpected Waves

Truth for Today: Matthew 14:30–31

"But when he saw the wind, he was afraid and, beginning to sink, cried out, 'Lord, save me!' Immediately Jesus reached out his hand and caught him."

---

*Y*ou were doing okay, until you weren't. It might have been a song, a date on the calendar, or a simple conversation that suddenly brought everything crashing down again. You didn't expect it. You thought you were past this part. You were walking on steady ground, and then, the wave hit.

Grief doesn't stay in organized stages. It comes in waves, some small and some overwhelming. A memory can ambush you, a moment of joy can quickly turn into tears. You're not doing anything wrong, you're human, and you're walking through a storm.

In Matthew 14, Peter stepped out of the boat to walk on water toward Jesus. For a moment he was focused, steady, and brave. But then he saw the wind, he felt the waves, and taking his eyes off of Jesus pulled him under.

That's what grief does. It distracts. It is disorienting. And it causes you to sink. But don't miss what happened next. Peter cried out, "Lord, save me!" And *immediately*, Jesus reached out and caught him. Not that you never sink. But when you do, Jesus is already reaching for you.

He doesn't shame Peter for sinking. He doesn't demand he try harder. He responds to Peter's cry with compassion and rescue. Jesus sank to the very bottom of death so He could raise you up from it. When that wave of sorrow comes, Jesus doesn't stand on the shore waiting for you to pull yourself together. He reminds you of His finished work.

He's already beside you, already reaching, already holding you up with His nail-pierced hands that have weathered every storm, including death.

So don't be afraid of the waves. Don't be ashamed when they come unexpectedly. Cry out. Lift your eyes. Let Him hold you again. You're not drowning—you're being loved.

Prayer

Lord, the waves of grief come when I least expect them. Sometimes I feel like I'm sinking. But thank You that You never let go of me. Thank You for sinking down to death and rising up to rescue me. Like Peter, I can cry out to You, and You'll always be there to raise me up.

Reflection Questions

1. What are some of the "memories" that have
   surprised you in this season?

   _____

   _____

   _____

   _____

   _____

2. How does Peter's story remind you of your need
   for Jesus in the middle of emotional chaos?

   _____

   _____

   _____

   _____

   _____

3. What would it look like to cry out to Jesus the next
   time the waves hit?

_____

_____

_____

_____

_____

_____

_____

_____

_____

_____

_____

_____

_____

Day 18 – Holidays, Anniversaries, and Dreaded Dates

Truth for Today: Romans 8:38–39

"For I am convinced that neither death nor life… nor anything else in all creation, will be able to separate us from the love of God that is in Christ Jesus our Lord."

The calendar reminds you, even when you don't want it to. The birthdays, anniversaries, the first Christmas without them, and the day they passed—the day everything changed. These dates once held joy; now they carry a heavy weight.

They sneak up on you, steal your sleep, and pierce your heart like an arrow. And sometimes, they make you wonder, will I always hurt like this? The short answer is, maybe not always like this—but yes, it may always leave a deep wound and scar. And that's okay. Love always leaves a mark.

Jesus died on a specific day. The Bible says that *"at just the right time, Christ died"* (Romans 5:6). After His resurrection, He showed the wounds in His hands and side—the wounds of love, the scars of purchase, the price He paid for the gift He gave.

Grief and sorrow on special days doesn't mean your faith is failing—it means your love was real, just like Jesus'.

That's why Romans 8 is such a powerful anchor. Romans doesn't offer shallow comfort, it declares confidence in an unbreakable love, a love that not even death can sever. Not even this day. Not even your worst memory. Not even your darkest moment. The love of Christ holds you when the day holds too much.

And if your loved one died in Christ, then His love still holds them, too. When the holiday table feels lonely, when the birthday goes uncelebrated, or when the weight of the anniversary feels like too much—let this be your hope… the same Jesus who wept at the tomb, is with you on each of these special dates.

He is not only the God of resurrection. He is the God of remembrance. He sees the dates, and knows the weight. One day, the calendar won't sting anymore. And in eternity, no date will be marked by death again. Until then, let the love of God in Christ Jesus be enough to carry you—now and all the way through eternity.

Prayer

Lord, these dates hurt, and at times I feel the loss more deeply. Thank You for reminding me that not even death can separate me from Your love. Help me walk through it with honesty and hope. Hold me in the pain, and remind me of the joy I have in knowing that You are always here.

Reflection Questions

1. What dates or holidays stir the deepest ache in you?

_____

_____

_____

_____

_____

2. How does knowing that nothing can separate you from Christ's love help you face them?

_____

_____

_____

_____

_____

3. What would it look like to honor those days with both grief and hope?

_____

_____

_____

_____

_____

_____

_____

_____

_____

_____

_____

_____

Day 19

Day 19 – Everyone's Moving On but Me

Truth for Today: Psalm 34:18

"The Lord is close to the brokenhearted and saves those who are crushed in spirit."

$\mathcal{I}$t seems like life around you has returned to normal. People are back to work, planning vacations, laughing in group chats, posting family pictures. And you… you're still trying to breathe. Still trying to get through the day. Still carrying the heartache that doesn't show up in photos.

It feels like everyone else has moved on, but you're stuck in the moment everything changed. Grief is lonely, and even with good people around you, there's a depth of sorrow that sometimes feels like it's yours to carry alone.

But the Bible says, *"The Lord is close to the brokenhearted."* He's not distant. He's not impatient with your process. He's not rolling His eyes while the rest of the world "moves on." He's near, still, today, in this slow, silent valley. And not just near—He saves those who are crushed in spirit. That's the gospel's language of love.

Jesus didn't come only for the strong and the joyful. He came for the brokenhearted and for those who are weeping. The ones who can't fake a smile.

He lived in our world, walked among our sorrows, and died to carry our greatest burden of sin and suffering. On the cross, He was not only crushed, but brokenhearted as the spear was thrust into His side—into His heart—so that yours could be healed.

So even if you feel stuck today, emotionally and mentally paralyzed while others keep going on, you're not behind. Your faith isn't failing. You're not forgotten. Grief doesn't come with a clock. Love doesn't expire after a month or a year. And healing doesn't come overnight, but over time—in the presence of the One who refuses to leave you.

Jesus isn't asking you to move on. He's inviting you to move with Him. And He promises to walk every step with you. Until your sorrow gives way to joy that no one can take away.

Prayer

Lord, it feels like the world has forgotten. Like everyone else has moved on while I'm still hurting. Thank You for not leaving me behind and for staying close when I feel crushed. Help me trust that You are walking with me, and that You'll never leave me.

Reflection Questions

1. In what ways have you felt "left behind" in your grief?

_____

_____

_____

_____

_____

2. How does Psalm 34:18 speak to your sense of loneliness?

_____

_____

_____

_____

_____

3. What does it mean that Jesus doesn't rush you but walks with you?

_____

_____

_____

_____

_____

_____

_____

_____

_____

_____

_____

_____

Day 20

Day 20 – When No One Understands

Truth for Today: Hebrews 4:15

"For we do not have a high priest who is unable to sympathize with our weaknesses, but one who in every respect has been tempted as we are, yet without sin."

$\mathcal{Y}$ou've heard kind words… but also hurtful ones. You've received hugs… but also silence. You've been told to stay strong, have faith, and "remember the good times."

But inside, you feel unseen, like no one really understands what this loss has done to you. And maybe… they don't. How could they?

Grief is deeply personal—it isn't just about who you lost, it's about how you loved them. What they meant to you, the void they filled, the future you imagined. So when people around you seem to expect you to "be okay," it makes the heartache even heavier.

But Hebrews 4:15 tells us that Christ is not a distant Savior. He is a compassionate High Priest who understands your weakness. He stepped into human space, time, and pain. He felt it. He carried it. He knows what it's like. He wept at a grave. He was abandoned by friends. He cried out in anguish. He bore the full weight of sorrow, and He did it for you. Jesus understands grief more deeply than anyone ever could.

And not only does He understand, it moved Him to act. He went to the cross to break death's grip. He rose from the grave to give you hope that loss is not the end of the journey. So even if no one else understands what you're walking through, Jesus does.

He doesn't just walk beside you, He lives in you. He sees and feels the weight you carry. And He carries it with you. When you feel alone, misunderstood, or invisible in your sorrow, turn to the One who truly sees. The Man of Sorrows is also the Savior of your soul, and He'll never let you go.

Prayer

Jesus, I feel like no one really understands what I'm going through, but You. Thank You for being the kind of Savior who stepped into suffering and walked through sorrow. I don't have to explain myself to You. You already know. Let me rest in Your promises and unfailing love.

Reflection Questions

1. In what ways have you felt misunderstood or alone in your grief?

_____

_____

_____

_____

_____

2. How does it affect your heart to know that Jesus truly understands your pain and meets you in it?

_____

_____

_____

_____

_____

3. What would it look like to open your heart to Him in a way others may not understand?

_____

_____

_____

_____

_____

_____

_____

_____

_____

_____

_____

_____

_____

Day 21 – Sleep, Eat, Breathe... Repeat

Truth for Today: Lamentations 3:22–23

"Because of the Lord's great love we are not consumed, for his compassions never fail. They are new every morning; great is your faithfulness."

---

*S*ome days, just getting out of bed is a victory. Grief has a way of draining your energy, your appetite, and your motivation. It's not just emotional, it's physical, mental, and spiritual.

You wake up tired. You go to bed tired. You wonder if life will ever feel like more than just surviving. Sleep, eat, breathe, repeat. You may feel like you're not doing enough, or like you're stuck in survival mode.

But today's Bible passage reminds you of this powerful truth—you're not being consumed by this. Not because of your strength. Not because you've figured out how to cope. But because God's mercies are new every morning. Every...single... morning.

Even the ones that feel like too much. Even the ones where the grief feels fresh again. Even the ones where you just go through the motions. Grief may still be present, but so is God's faithfulness.

The same God who saw you through yesterday will meet you in this moment with exactly what you need. Not more than you need, not less. Just enough mercy for today. When Israel was wandering in the wilderness, God didn't drop a month's supply of manna all at once. He gave them fresh bread each morning (Exodus 16). Enough for the day, not stored up, but steady.

In Christ, you have access to that same daily bread. The One who came down from heaven like manna and was broken for you. The Bread of Life is your Bread for Life. He is your living water. He is the strength for today, the hope in your fatigue, and real love that never fails. So if today looks like just getting through it, that's okay.

If today means eating, breathing, surviving, and nothing more, that's okay. You're not behind or broken beyond repair. You're still here, still held, still loved. And tomorrow's mercies will meet you again—they are new every morning.

Prayer

Lord, sometimes I feel like all I'm doing is barely getting by. But thank You that Your mercies are new each morning—even on the hardest days. Help me stop striving and start depending on You. Give me grace for this moment, and peace to rest in Your faithful love.

Reflection Questions

1. Have you felt guilty about "just surviving" in your grief?

_____

_____

_____

_____

_____

2. What does it mean that God's mercies are new every morning, even in sadness?

_____

_____

_____

_____

_____

3. How can you lean on Jesus for daily strength instead of trying to power through?

_____

_____

_____

_____

_____

_____

_____

_____

_____

_____

_____

_____

Day 22 – It's Okay to Laugh Again

Truth for Today: Ecclesiastes 3:4

"A time to weep and a time to laugh, a time to mourn and a time to dance."

The first time you laugh after a loss can feel wrong. Like a betrayal. Like you're moving on too fast. Like you've forgotten someone you promised you never would. Grief plays tricks on your heart and mind. It says that healing is disloyal. That joy means you didn't love them enough. That laughter is disrespectful to your loss.

But the Bible says there is a time to weep and a time to laugh. That's not a command to fake it or force it. It's a reminder that joy and sorrow can exist together—even in the valley of mourning, God can surprise you with laughter again.

Grief changes you, of course, but it doesn't erase the image of God in you. And God is a God of joy. He created smiles, jokes, friendships, moments that warm your heart and lift the burdens even for a short time. That's not betrayal. That's God's grace at work for you and in you.

Jesus was the Man of Sorrows, but He also attended weddings, and enjoyed meals with friends. He rejoiced in the Spirit. And one day, when all is made new, He will throw a feast, full of joy, singing, and dancing (Isaiah 25:6–8; Revelation 19:9). Don't feel guilty when the corner of your heart lights up again. It doesn't mean you've moved on. It means God is still moving in you.

The gospel isn't just that Jesus died—it's that He rose again. Resurrection is joy coming out of sorrow. Laughter returning after weeping. Light shining after darkness. And if you belong to Him, that resurrection life is already at work in you, even in grief. So yes, laugh. Laugh without guilt.

Laugh because the One who bore your sorrow has also restored your hope. And joy—real joy—is proof that love never fails.

Prayer

Jesus, I've felt unsure about joy. Afraid to laugh, afraid to move forward. But You are the God of resurrection, and You give joy in the middle of sorrow. Help me to receive Your gift of grace, not guilt. Let laughter remind me that love still lives, and that You are making all things new.

Reflection Questions

1. Have you felt guilty for laughing or enjoying moments in your grief?

_____

_____

_____

_____

_____

2. How does Ecclesiastes 3 free you to experience both sorrow and joy?

_____

_____

_____

_____

_____

3. How is God inviting you to receive joy as part of healing?

_____

_____

_____

_____

_____

_____

_____

_____

_____

_____

_____

_____

Day 23 – When Others Say the Wrong Thing

Truth for Today: Proverbs 18:21

"The tongue has the power of life and death, and those who love it will eat its fruit."

They meant well, but their words cut deep. Maybe they tried to comfort you and said something careless. Maybe they offered clichés instead of compassion. Maybe they gave you advice when you needed a hug. Or maybe they said nothing at all, and their silence was worse.

Grief is hard enough, but when people say the wrong thing, it adds another layer of pain, frustration, confusion, and sometimes resentment. Proverbs 18:21 reminds us that words carry weight. They can lift a heart or crush a spirit. They can bring healing or deepen the wound. And in grief, the wrong words can echo long after the conversation ends.

So what do you do?

Be honest about the pain. You don't have to pretend it didn't hurt, but try to think the best of others, even when their words fall short. They did the best they could under the circumstances. Even Jesus was hurt by the words and actions of others. He was misunderstood, dismissed, and wounded deeply by those close to Him.

But look to the One whose Word never fails. When people's words fail you, God's Word heals you. People may offer shallow phrases, but when God speaks—it penetrates down to the heart and soul. They may be uncomfortable with your sorrow, but God draws near to the brokenhearted. They may want you to move on, but God is patient, kind, and present in every moment.

And here's the gospel that brings hope, Jesus didn't just endure painful words, He endured the cross and spoke with spikes in His hands and feet. *"Father, forgive them, for they do not know what they are doing."*

Those words weren't careless—but they were costly. They declared your forgiveness, your healing, your future. And no misguided comment can cancel what He accomplished for you on the cross. So when others say the wrong thing, think the best of them and return to the Word of God. It restores, heals, and reminds you that you are seen, loved, and cherished in Christ.

And today, you may even find the grace to forgive as you've been forgiven. Forgive those who didn't know what to say. They're hurting too. And the same gospel that comforts you—is powerful enough to sustain you.

Prayer

Father, some words have hurt more than helped. I feel misunderstood, dismissed, or judged. But Your Word is living and active to help and heal. Thank You for speaking life into me when others didn't know how. Help me listen to Your words above all, and to think the best of others when they stumble over their own.

Reflection Questions

1. Have you been hurt by someone's words (or silence) during your grief?

_____

_____

_____

_____

2. What does God's Word say that people may have failed to say?

_____

_____

_____

_____

3. How can the truth of the gospel help you forgive as
   you've been forgiven?

   _____

   _____

   _____

   _____

   _____

   _____

   _____

   _____

   _____

   _____.

Day 24 – Carrying Their Legacy

Truth for Today: Hebrews 12:1

"Therefore, since we are surrounded by such a great cloud of witnesses, let us throw off everything that hinders... and let us run with perseverance the race marked out for us."

---

*T*hey're not here to finish what they started. The conversations, the dreams, the time spent together, were all cut short. And now you're left holding the memories, the values, the impact of a life that mattered deeply to you.

So what now?

What do you do with their legacy? Hebrews 12:1 paints a picture of those who have gone before us, whose lives now bear witness to God's faithfulness. Their race is over, but yours is still unfolding.

That doesn't mean you forget them—it means you keep going because of them. You don't carry their legacy to prove anything. You carry it as an act of love, an extension of their impact in your life. Their race may be finished, but you're still running, still breathing, still here for a purpose.

And the gospel gives you more than memories to hold onto. It gives you hope to run and finish your race. Like

Jesus, the One who ran His race perfectly, is now the Author and Finisher of your faith (Hebrews 12:2).

Because of Jesus' finished race and present help, you don't run aimlessly—He runs with you and strengthens you. So what does it look like to carry their legacy?

Maybe it's telling their stories to the next generation. Maybe it's showing kindness the way they did. Maybe it's finishing a project they started, or living with the same faith they had.

It's not about replacing them. It's about honoring them through the way you live. But ultimately, your race isn't about them—it's about Christ. He's not just your finish line, but also your plumb line. He is your strength, your prize, and the anchor of your soul.

And when you finally reach the end of your own race, you'll be reunited with all those who are in Christ. Until that day, you run with the memory of their love in your heart, and the power of the gospel in your soul.

Prayer

Jesus, I want to carry their legacy well. I miss them. I feel the weight of what they left behind. Help me run my race with perseverance. Help me honor their life, but most of all, help me follow You with my whole heart. Thank You that I'm not alone, and that You give strength for each day and for every step.

Reflection Questions

1. What qualities or values from your loved one do you hope to carry forward?

_____

_____

_____

_____

_____

2. How does knowing their race is finished help you keep going in yours?

_____

_____

_____

_____

_____

3. In what ways can you live out both their legacy and the calling Christ has for you?

_____

_____

_____

_____

_____

_____

_____

_____

_____

_____

_____

_____

_____

Day 25 – What If I Forget Them?

Truth for Today: Isaiah 49:16

"See, I have engraved you on the palms of my hands; your walls are ever before me."

$\mathcal{Y}$ou're scared the memories will fade. That one day you won't remember the sound of their voice, the way they laughed, the small things that made them who they are.

You fear time will dull the details. That life will go on, and leave them behind. Even in grief, there's another kind of loss that creeps in: the fear of forgetting. Love does not depend on a perfect memory.

And even when your mind grows tired or your heart grows weary, God never forgets. Isaiah 49:16 gives us a powerful image.

God says, *"I have engraved you on the palms of my hands."*

Not written in pencil or pen, not marked temporarily, but forever engraved in the "palms of my hands." Picture the wounds in Jesus' hands. See Him hanging there on the cross—for you, with you in His heart, with you on His mind. This is new covenant love.

Is This the End?

Your loved one was known by Him too. Held by Him. Their life, their breath, their moments—engraved on His hands. And if they belonged to Jesus, those very hands—the hands pierced on the cross—welcomed them home.

Because of the gospel, the memory you're trying so hard to preserve is already held perfectly in eternity. Nothing of eternal value is ever truly lost. Jesus didn't just die to defeat sin and death—He rose to secure life forever. That means the person you miss so deeply is not forgotten by God, and one day, in Christ, you will see them again.

So don't carry the burden of keeping every memory perfectly sharp or always in the forefront of your mind. Rest in the truth that what you forget, God remembers. And what He remembers, He redeems. Let that be enough for today.

Prayer

Father, I'm afraid of forgetting. The details, the voice, the moments. But You don't forget. You've engraved their life on Your hands, and You've engraved me there too. Help me to rest in Your faithfulness, not my memory. Thank You that nothing is lost in Your love.

Reflection Questions

1. What specific memory are you most afraid of losing?

_____

_____

_____

_____

2. How does Isaiah 49:16 comfort you when you feel the pressure to "hold on"?

_____

_____

_____

_____

3. What would it look like to rest in God's perfect memory instead of your own?

_____

_____

_____

_____

_____

_____

_____

_____

_____

_____

_____

_____

Day 26 – Healing Is Not Betrayal

Truth for Today: Philippians 3:13–14

"Forgetting what is behind and straining toward what is ahead, I press on toward the goal to win the prize for which God has called me heavenward in Christ Jesus."

---

*Y*ou're starting to laugh again. You've had a few good days. Maybe you've made a decision, a change, or even a plan you didn't think you could make. And suddenly, you feel guilty. Am I moving on too fast? Am I betraying their memory?

You don't want to forget. You don't want to leave them behind. And here's the truth—healing is not betrayal. Pressing forward doesn't mean you're letting go of love or memories. It means you're learning to carry that love differently, inside your heart instead of beside you.

When Paul writes about "forgetting what is behind," he's talking about our past life before knowing Christ—not erasing our family and friends we love. He's calling us to stop living in the past so we can walk forward in what Christ has ahead. And in grief, that means allowing God to gently rebuild what sorrow broke.

Jesus never asked you to forget your loved ones—but He does call you to remember Him. And remembering Him

Is This the End?

means remembering His cross, where He bore your weight and your sorrow, and His empty tomb, where He secured life for you.

Healing doesn't mean you'll never cry again. It doesn't mean their absence stops hurting. It simply means Christ is doing what only He can do, renewing your heart, restoring your joy, and reminding you that you still have a purpose.

If your loved one could speak from eternity, they would tell you: Keep going. Keep living. Keep loving. Keep running your race. Because this isn't the end, and your story isn't over.

Let go of the lie that healing is disloyal. Jesus is the one who gave you that love in the first place, and He's the one walking you toward restoration. So press on. Not to forget, but to live. To trust. To hope again. Because Jesus has more for you, and His love never asks you to choose between memory and healing—it gives you both.

Prayer

Jesus, part of me is afraid to heal. I don't want to forget. I don't want to dishonor what they meant to me. But thank You for reminding me that healing is not betrayal—it's grace. Help me press on, not because I've stopped loving, but because You're still leading. I trust You with my heart, my grief, and my future.

Reflection Questions

1. In what ways have you felt guilt for healing or "moving forward"?

_____

_____

_____

_____

_____

2. How does Philippians 3 encourage you to press on without letting go of love?

_____

_____

_____

_____

_____

Is This the End?

3. What might it look like to embrace healing as a gift from God, not a betrayal?

_____

_____

_____

_____

_____

_____

_____

_____

_____

_____

_____

_____

Day 27 – Light in the Darkness

Truth for Today: 2 Corinthians 4:6

"For God, who said, 'Let light shine out of darkness,' made his light shine in our hearts to give us the light of the knowledge of God's glory displayed in the face of Christ."

---

*G*rief has a way of making everything feel darker. The nights feel longer. The mornings feel heavier. The joy you once felt seems like a distant memory. Sometimes it's not just a dark day—it's a dark season. And it can feel like the light will never break through again.

But then comes this stunning verse—the same God who spoke light into the darkness at creation is the same God who now shines His light into your heart. That means you are not stuck in this darkness. Not forgotten in it, and never alone walking through it.

When Paul wrote these words to the Corinthians, he was reminding them of something deeper than just emotional hope. He was pointing them to the gospel.

Christ, the Light of the World, has already entered the darkest night—the deepest sorrow on the cross—and defeated it through the power of His resurrection. That same powerful light now lives in you. Not a flicker, nor a spark.

Even when you're surrounded by shadows, He is still the Light shining in your darkness. And here's the beauty of the gospel—God doesn't demand you "find the light" on your own. He is the Light of Life living in you.

Christ's light is not dependent on your strength, it's dependent on His grace. So today, if the weight is heavy and the light seems dim, remember that Jesus is the Light of the World and in Him there is no darkness at all.

Prayer

Jesus, sometimes I feel surrounded by darkness, grief, confusion, and sadness I can't put into words. But You are the Light of the World, remind me that no darkness is too deep for You. Thank You for the cross, Your resurrection, and for being The Light of life and The Truth that sets me free.

Reflection Questions

    1.   What part of your grief still feels like darkness?

    2.   How does it encourage you to know that Jesus the Light of the World lives in you?

3. What does it mean that Christ's presence and light are guiding you today?

_____

_____

_____

_____

_____

_____

_____

_____

_____

_____

_____

_____

_____

Day 28 – A Place Where There's No More Death

Truth for Today: Revelation 21:4

"He will wipe every tear from their eyes. There will be no more death or mourning or crying or pain, for the old order of things has passed away."

Some wounds don't fully heal in this life. Some tears don't dry completely. Some pain remains, even years after the loss. And yet, this is not the end. God promises a day is coming—a real day—when He will wipe every tear from your eyes.

Not symbolically, but physically, personally, and tenderly. Because your tears matter to Him. Your pain matters to Him. You matter to Him. Revelation 21 gives us a glimpse of the future Jesus purchased for us through His death and resurrection. A place with no more death, because death itself will once and for all be swallowed up.

No more mourning, because everything broken will be made whole. No more crying or pain, because God Himself will dwell with His people, forever. This is not religious wishful thinking—this is gospel reality. Secured by Christ, paid for in blood, and guaranteed by an empty tomb.

Jesus didn't rise from the dead to offer a comforting thought, He rose to defeat death permanently. That means grief doesn't have the last word. Cancer doesn't get the final word. Accidents, tragedy, even time itself, none of it wins—eternity wins.

And if you're in Christ, you win with Him. So today, let your heart ache if it needs to. Let the tears fall again if they come. But do not grieve as if this world is all there is. Do not grieve as if this goodbye is forever, because in Christ, death is just the beginning of eternity with Him.

This life may feel long, but eternity is longer. And every moment of sorrow here will be swallowed up by the joy that's coming. That's your hope. Not just healing, but home.

Prayer

Father, I long for that day, no more death, no more pain, no more goodbyes. Thank You for giving me this promise in Christ. Help me hold on when the sorrow is deep. Thank You that Jesus rose again, and that because of Him, I have a future beyond the grave.

Reflection Questions

1. What part of this promise from Revelation gives you the most hope today?

_____

_____

_____

_____

_____

2. How does knowing death will one day be destroyed reshape how you grieve now?

_____

_____

_____

_____

_____

3. Do you believe that, in Christ, this is not the end? Why, or why not?

_____

_____

_____

_____

_____

_____

_____

_____

_____

_____

_____

_____

Day 29 – Reunion Ahead

Truth for Today: 1 Thessalonians 4:17

"And so we will be with the Lord forever."

---

*Y*ou've said goodbye. You've wept at the grave. You've sat in silence, aching to hear their voice one more time. And deep down, you wonder, will I ever see them again? If your loved one died in Christ, the answer is yes—a loud, heaven backed, blood-bought yes.

1 Thessalonians 4 paints one of the clearest pictures of what's coming for those who belong to Jesus. Paul says, "the dead in Christ will rise, and then we who are still alive will be caught up with them, and so we will be with the Lord forever."

Notice that word: we. Not just you. Not just them, but we. Together, whole, home, forever. This is our hope. This is resurrection truth. It's guaranteed.

The same Jesus who walked out of the tomb will return for you. And when He does, He will reunite His people, body, spirit, and soul. Earth and heaven, you and them. The reunion is real. Not a dream. Not a vague spiritual fantasy. But a literal, joyful, eternal gathering of those made alive in Christ.

Is This the End?

And even better, we'll be with the Lord—forever. No more sin. No more sorrow. No more separation. Just worship, wonder, and unending joy in the presence of the Savior who made it all possible. That's why grief is never the full story for the believer. Yes, we mourn. But we mourn with hope (1 Thess. 4:13).

Because the same God who received your loved one will one day call you home too. And when He does, there will be no more goodbyes, only "welcome back." So look ahead—and let this truth comfort your heart today.

Prayer

Jesus, I long for that reunion. I miss them so much. But thank You for the promise that in You, this goodbye is not forever. Thank You that death cannot separate what You have redeemed. Keep my heart anchored in the hope of seeing them—and seeing You—face to face, forever.

Reflection Questions

1. How does the promise of reunion give you
   strength in your current grief?

_____

_____

_____

_____

_____

2. What do you imagine that moment will be like,
   when you see them again?

_____

_____

_____

_____

_____

3. How does the hope of being with Jesus forever shape how you live today?

_____

_____

_____

_____

_____

_____

_____

_____

_____

_____

_____

_____

_____

Day 30 – Not the End, But the Beginning

Truth for Today: Romans 8:18

"I consider that our present sufferings are not worth comparing with the glory that will be revealed in us."

$\mathcal{Y}$ou've walked through the valley. You've asked the hard questions, cried the painful tears, wrestled with the silence, and wondered if life could ever be whole again. And maybe you still feel the weight. That's okay. But hear this clearly friend—this is not the end; it never was.

The world says death is the end of the road, but the gospel says otherwise. Because of Jesus, death has been defeated—not merely delayed. Because of Jesus, this suffering, as heavy and real as it is, is not the end, but the middle of the story.

Paul writes in Romans 8 that our present sufferings aren't even worth comparing to what's coming. Not because our suffering isn't great, but because the glory ahead is so much greater. And that glory is not vague or far off. It's Christ Himself. Face to face. Whole. Healed. Home.

No more death, no more grief, no more questions. Just Him, and those we've lost in Him, alive, forever. That's your ending and your beginning. The cross looked like the end,

Is This the End?

but it was the start of redemption. The tomb looked final, but it turned into resurrection power and new life.

And your sorrow, as dark as it may be now, will one day give way to light you can't imagine. Jesus didn't save you to leave you in the valley. He saved you to bring you all the way home.

And so, until then, keep grieving honestly, keep remembering their love deeply, keep living purposefully, and keep hoping boldly—because the best is yet to come, and it has already been secured by Jesus' nail-scarred hands.

Prayer

Jesus, thank You for walking with me through every step of this valley. Thank You for carrying my pain, my questions, my tears, and for giving me eternal hope. I believe this is not the end. Because of You, forever is coming—and it will be worth the wait. Resurrection is coming, and I will see You face to face, and be reunited with loved ones forever.

Reflection Questions

1. How has your perspective on grief and eternity shifted through these 30 days?

_____

_____

_____

_____

2. What part of "the glory to come" gives you the most peace right now?

_____

_____

_____

_____

3. How can you walk forward with hope today, knowing this is not the end?

_____

_____

_____

_____

_____

_____

_____

_____

_____

_____

_____

_____

_____

Dear friend,

Whether you are alone in life or surrounded by family, you are not finished until your final breath. As long as God gives you life, He still has purpose for you—especially as part of the body of Christ.

Somebody needs your story.
Somebody needs your compassion.
Somebody needs your love.
Somebody needs your ear.
Somebody needs someone to mourn with.

And you could be that person—right where God has placed you.

So whether you have a year to live—make it count. Make an impact. Love others well.

Invitation

If this devotional has encouraged you, I'd love to hear from you. How is God working in your life? How has this devotional blessed you? How can I pray for you or serve you?

Your story matters. Your testimony of God's grace could be the encouragement someone else needs to keep going. Feel free to share your thoughts, prayer requests, or what God is doing in your life—I'd be honored to listen, pray, and celebrate with you.

Other Books by Erick Hurt

Coming Soon

- **What Good Am I?:** 30 Days of Hope for a Life That Matters
- **This is Real Love:** A 30-Day Devotional on True Love
- **Be Sober Minded:** A 30-Day Devotional on Transforming Your Mind
- **Let Freedom Ring:** A 30-Day Devotional on Law vs. Grace

For more updates, visit ErickHurt.com

Group Leader's Guide: Is This the End?

Purpose of the Group

To comfort those grieving in the truth of the gospel, renew their hope in Christ, and help them walk in daily in the gospel that can heal their wounds, encourage their hearts, and anchor their hope in their time of loss.

How to Use This Devotional in a Group

1. Weekly Gatherings (Recommended)
- Meet once a week to discuss the 7 devotionals from that week.

- Choose a quiet space where everyone can share comfortably.

2. Everyone Reads Daily
- Group members read one devotional each day (30 days total).

- Encourage members to write in their books—prayers, notes, and reflections.

3. Focus on Jesus
- Each session is centered on the finished work of Christ.

- Help participants see how every lesson points to Him—His death, resurrection, and their new life in Him.

Suggested Weekly Group Format (60–75 minutes)

1. Welcome & Prayer (5 minutes)

Begin with a warm welcome and a short prayer. Ask God to guide your time together.

2. Check-In (10–15 minutes)

Ask each person to share briefly how the week went and how the devotionals impacted them.
Example question: "What truth encouraged or challenged you this week?"

3. Scripture Focus (10 minutes)

Choose one or two key Scriptures from the past week's devotionals. Read them aloud together and ask what stood out or how they point to Christ.

4. Group Discussion (25–30 minutes)

Use the core discussion questions below to guide conversation. Encourage honesty, listening, and gospel-centered sharing.

5. Application & Prayer (15 minutes)

Close by asking: "How can we pray for you?" Spend time praying for one another, focusing on gospel hope, freedom, and transformation.

Core Discussion Questions (repeat weekly)

1. What truth stood out most to you this week?

2. Where did you feel challenged, or encouraged?

3. How did the gospel become more real to you?

4. What is God inviting you to give up or believe?

5. How can we pray for you this week?

Leader Encouragement

You and I are not the experts—Jesus is. Be a good listener, quick to listen and slow to speak. Try not to be a fixer. Stay focused on the gospel, not behavior change. The goal is heart transformation through the finished work of Christ.

www.ingramcontent.com/pod-product-compliance
Lightning Source LLC
Chambersburg PA
CBHW060621130626
46555CB00002B/601